FlowerSong Press
McAllen, Texas 78501
Copyright © 2020 by Anatalia Vallez

ISBN: 978-1-7345617-3-9

Published by FlowerSong Press
in the United States of America.
www.flowersongbooks.com

Set in Adobe Garamond Pro

Cover design and art by john jairo valencia
Typeset by Matthew Revert
Author photograph by Tara Deaton

No part of this book may be reproduced without written permission from the publisher.

All inquiries and permission requests should be addressed to the Publisher.

to all survivors of violence—
may we reclaim our power
and our narratives

y para las mujeres que me rebozaron

Roots

bond
vínculo
ceding
ruler in the mirror
strawberry fields are forever
descansa conmigo
La Doña
pero me entendiste
tres de julio
ancestral system of measurement
papalos in my backpack
in this one

Core

Healthy is a colonizing word
Stages
sardines in a tin can
roundup
manos a la obra
I'll probably bleed at the Border™
La Trenzuda
misogyny invites itself in with a joke
I forgot to ask my therapist
HALT
guilty
endurance
manifesto
document it
beauty is in the eye of my beloved

Heart

craving citrus
how to have a good cry
Pink Lights Up
mojito
dis en tangled
without over apologizing
I improvised a monologue
stop raising him, he's not your son
the last fuckboi
La Sirena
breaking patterns, leaving notes
mosaic
heart

Head

shedding
Y Si No Me Quieren
to this body
I didn't want her to die
there's a cumbia in here for you
call it joy
evolving
for folks that are soft
mi abuela se sabe una canción
my grandma knows a song
una semilla
community call-in

Roots
noun.
the part of a plant that attaches to the ground or to a support, typically underground, conveying water and nourishment to the rest of the plantbond[1] ; the part you are told to cut off in case no one else has already done it for you.

---

[1] Merriam-Webster online definition

bond

as a fetus my mother inhaled love
it lingered in her vocal chords
then traveled to her stomach
through her umbilical cord
and into me
it now lives between my stomach and diaphragm

Perhaps that's why I exist
to exhale what was trapped in my mother's throat

vínculo

cuando aún estaba en su vientre
mi mamá inspiró amor
perduró en sus cuerdas vocales
se desenvolvió en su estómago
y viajó por la cuerda umbilical
hasta llegar a mi
ahorra vive entre mi estómago y diafragma

Tal vez por eso existo
para exhalar lo que se detuvo en su garganta

ceding

she was so small. so tiny. her limbs were all there though.
he'd check several times:
two eyes, two arms, ten toes and ten fingers.

he felt this love rush through his bloodstream.
he knew he was going to have an apology slide out of his knees.
because no one was going to take her away.

he memorized her face.
just in case.
as he got ready to hand her over she began to move her mouth.

cooing

    qué quieres mi vida
        the baby communicated
        what she'd heard for nine months

  cooing

    qué quieres mi cielo
        the baby called out
        his anger

  cooing

    que paso
        the baby asked,
        "will you always be this soft with me?"

  cooing

    until he handed her over

ruler in the mirror

I'm sitting on the edge of the bathtub
pretending to brush my hair
watching her look intently in the mirror
she takes out a comb and delicately parts her hair

raises a tweezer to her brows
while the curling iron heats up
sharpens a red lip liner
raises the music
hums as she powders her face
studying every pore and freckle

looks into the eyes of her father
the nose of her mother
takes the curler to her bangs and creates an arch
shoulders back

powerful
in control
practicing the skills of a painter
her face is her pallet

sweeps her hair into a perfectly symmetrical work of art
sprays hairspray to secure her crown and departs

no matter how out of control life situations may be
she is the almighty ruler of herself, after all

she has fought hard to be in control of her body and mind

she kisses my forehead before she leaves to face the day
I almost drop my brush

what an honor
to be raised by someone who reclaims
her divinity after being mutilated
and what a privilege
to feel the ripple effects of self-love

strawberry fields are forever

legs and arms aching
I would run to the door excited for an embrace

they'd back away
no mija

my father denies it now
my uncles chuckle and grab another beer
my grandfathers hum under their breath
but strawberry fields are forever

I'd lift my hands against theirs
was it dirt or were their hands that
brown
        splintered
                broken
                        strong
                                comforting
able to hold my weight
tap their fingers to Ritchie Valens
spin records on the weekends
then bend their backs against a hot califas sun on monday

blood disguised by the sweet juice
mixed with a days sweat
was our normal

on the occasional day when carts were hauled in
I cheerfully scarfed them down and giggled
a child too young to perceive
strawberry fields are forever

descansa conmigo

I listen to my grandmother's heartbeat telling me stories of heartbreaks and triumphs she has kept below the earth. Every morning she imagines every possible storm as she wraps her back with a bandage. She holds the weight of the world with a thousand ropes, but at her eighty-seven years of age her body is begging her to let go. Her back is deforming and her organs could be affected next. We sit at the dining table while my mom holds my grandmother's x-rays to the light.
She cries, we all cry. As night falls I ask Tonantzin why mothers must suffer so much. Why womxns bodies are treated like machines running on little sleep and half-mouthed yes's and more's. One day abuelita confessed that she cries worrying about how the world will treat her granddaughters. I don't dare tell her about my body issues. How I've been taught my self-worth is valued by how others see me. Can I tell her to put herself before others if I'm still learning what that looks like for me?

I look at my grandmother's eyes and see myself reflected in her. A deep peace sweeps over me. My grandmother and I can be very set in our ways. But we aren't afraid of learning. As she sleeps, I whisper to her heart, "Let the world take care of itself. Love yourself and I promise—
I will too"

La Doña

Dicen que La Doña cantaba cuando era joven
y a veces se alcanza a escuchar desde el parque
como esfuerza su voz
como cada fin de palabra suena como un llanto
la tristeza que se traga
Ahoga su canto hasta que
el silencio la calla

sus hijos, todos hombres
son su todo
aunque estén resentidos
algún día me agradecerán

Dicen que ya está cansada
que sus gritos no son los de antes
cuando les regañaba a sus hijos por sus travesuras
o cuando asustaba a las novias
es por su bien

Dicen que cuando La Doña se enojaba
toda la cuadra corría hacia sus casas
les voy a enseñar a ser hombres

Ahora se queda en casa
camina agarrándose de la pared o de lo que pueda
su baño está lleno de medicamentos que le manda su hijo del
Norte

Si me quieren
Si — me quieren
Si, ¿me quieren?

trata de callar la voz de duda
la misma voz que hace muchos años la convenció
a no seguir su sueño de ser artista
Cucurrucucú, paloma
Cucurrucucú, no llores
Las piedras jamás, paloma
Qué van a saber de amores
Cucurrucucú,
Cucurrucucú
Paloma, ya no llores

pero me entendiste

My brother runs around covering the holes in our words
    "No se dice, vinites, se dice veniste"
        my sister excavates,
            "como se dice te quiero mucho"
                "te makti nimitzneki",
my grandma replies
    "abuelita, y como se dice abuelita"
        "no koltsi"
"abuelita"
        "que"
"Te makti nimitzneki, no koltsi"

My grandpa only swears in nahuatl.
His favorite line in english is: "gimme one beer"
My uncle puts his english in a blender, sprinkles it in his tacos.
My mom adds a few drops in her perfume.
    "Oh really?" she replies to the Mexican taxi driver.

I will forever be mocked for referring to a piece of bread
by the brand: la tia rosa
    "La tía rosa no se vende niña", the store owner said
mockingly
I cried, my stomach still craving the mini buttered croissants.
All I took home was shame for not speaking *right*.

they say: speak the truth, even if your voice shakes
and I acknowledge

our broken words
these collected
overflowing languages
are our earth shaking truths
refusing to be put to sleep

tres de julio

le llamaron loca por criar a sus hijos sin un padre
le dijeron que no podía sola
¿qué va a decir la gente?
juzgaron, criticaron

hasta familiares le dejaron de llamar
no sabían si teníamos donde dormir
o comida para comer
pero aquí estamos más de 15 años después

por eso, no me asusta si me llaman loca
por creer en mí misma
si mi mamá pudo sola
sobresalir, luchar día con día, ¿yo por qué no?

no se necesita un padre para criar una familia
se necesita amor, ternura y atención
yo me surtí porque tuve lo triple
de mi mamá y mis dos hermanos

ancestral system of measurement

we use sardine cans to measure bulk food
with the palm of our hands we measure salt
with the quantity value of un monton we measure work
time is measured in ache

there are two time periods
B.D. and A.D.
before and after
displacement

with our index finger pointing up we measure a person's height
the quantity of un chingo is how we measure commitment
we count the distance of going around the sun and all the planets
as the measurement for our love
which is roughly about un chingo y un monton

in Spanish, te quiero means:
I like you
I desire you
I care for you
te amo means:
I love you
but offers no quantity or distance
So if you tell someone, te quiero un chingo y un montón
now that's a lot of love

papalos in my backpack
an ode to everything that didn't go to waste

The cement my uncle used to cover up a spot on the wall
The jeans that were cut to make my brother's clothes
The tortillas my mom took when she crossed the border
The egg shells my grandma uses to fertilize the soil
The discarded cardboard my grandpa recycles
The thrift clothes my sister tailors to her size
The books my brother finds and mends
The papalos in my backpack we ate for dinner
The laughter coming out of the gaps in our teeth
The tears we envelope in grief and send with an *I miss you*
The rage in our questions
The questions in our rage

the pauses between our stories

Your forgiveness
Your unmatched socks
Your single earring
Your seamless confidence
Your love
Your laughter
Your tears
Your rage
Your rage
Look around you

chances are
there is still something
worth saving

in this one
After Franny Choi

I didn't have to seal the envelope of self-deprecation or strain my back to be a good worker. No. In this one fever didn't hit the natives. We didn't have to sell our land for pharmaceutical drugs. The colonizing gaze was punishable with death. In this one, we didn't have to prove our pain. We wouldn't be called crazy or scary if we lost our cool in public because it would be seen as an energetic wave, a pulse, a moment, an effect and not a cause for violence. In this one we didn't have to lock our doors or our hearts because the most beautiful present someone could give us would be an invitation
to open it

Chilacachapa, Guerrero, 1979

Core
noun.
the dense central region of a planet, especially the nickel–iron inner part of the earth; the muscles of the torso, especially the lower back and abdominal area, which assists in the maintenance of good posture, balance[1]; the part everyone cares about for aesthetics not functionality; what you start using when you realize you don't need a microphone to be heard.

Healthy is a colonizing word

we overcompensated
ate and drank
as if we could slurp people fat shaming in one gulp of milk tea boba
chicken strips and artisanal cheese and all the things our mothers begged us to stop eating
so we wouldn't look like them

I flirt with decolonizing my diet
but I fear that my skin would split open and my organs turned to stone
for I would be seen all full and round
and be called Goddess of Expression
so I eat what is on the dollar menu

until I forget what I was angry about
and the plate in front of me is a trail of
saguaros in the desert
I pat my luscious grease glossed lips with a napkin
a blood red color comes off but I'm not scared

we're vegetarian now, except when rent is due
last week we put a whole can of chipotle sauce in black bean burgers so they looked like adobe my grandfather made
as the heat bit the tips of our tongues
I could feel my pores glowing

my senses awaken
we hissed and ahh'd the malos aires away
laughed as tears ran down our cheeks
then split a chocolate bar

Stages
Morning. A young girl is talking to her sister who refuses to get out of bed

What are you doing? Get up. What, are you seven? Can't you see it's daylight? Get up! Get ready. It's a new day. Come on, let's go. What hurts? Come on. What, do you want me to brush your teeth for you? No? I won't let you stay in bed. Get up. Come on. Oh, fine. I'll make you pancakes. Ay, come on. Get up. Come—
goes to grab her but her sister yells in pain
What? What! Mom! What's wrong? Let's go sing songs, dance and talk. Let's skip in the park. Move like the animals move. We can go down the slide in Tewinkle. Run through the sprinklers at Valencia Street. Let's go. Go to Christine's house. Stop pretending. I hate you! Why are you faking? You are scaring me. It's like you aren't my sister anymore. Stop it. Stop it now. Get up and tell me what's wrong. I'll take you to karaoke, ballet, dance... Whatever. I'll buy you all the chili cheddar fries in the world. I promise. Just stop laying there. Stop it. What? What is that? Where are we? No, no more tests. I'm tired of tests. What is wrong with her?
paces back and forth
She's okay. She's okay. She's okay.
a doctor comes in and makes an announcement
You mean. What? No, no, no, no.
the next morning
Morning. Come on. I'll help you up.

sardines in a tin can

babysitters running late to Anaheim Hills
cooks nodding off from their night shift in Huntington Beach
kids from the brown neighborhoods
rerouting to the good white schools in Tustin
bump and push and shove
for a little space to

breathe

silent screams from adults
loud ones from kids
right leg forward
if the brakes hit hard
left leg back
to support the impact

energy colliding in the city

elders
children
mothers
confused adolescents
ignored by city planners
neglected
left with nowhere to sit

It's just not part of the plan
until they are killed like sardines in a tin can

roundup

99 bottles
of beer on the wall
99 bottles
my uncle is gone

you take one down
throw him around
98 more
to throw in a stall

no more bottles
of beer on the wall
thousands snatched
in plain sight

you go to the store
catch some more
now you have plenty
to freely exploit

manos a la obra

born and raised en el Sur de Califas
I am a reflection
I am a product
I am a witness
                         to the struggle
                         the pain
                         the agony
                         the stress
                         the anger
                         the insecurity
                         the duality
                         of Borders™
                         finite

                                                         racism
                                                         resentment
                                                         political strategy
                                                         target
        like chess pieces on the untouched landscape
escape?   escape?   escape where?
this will never be your home
get used to living in doubt   in fear
                                                     in animosity
                                                       in grief
                                                  pay with blood
                         sacrifice yourself for this country
                         no one asks you how you are doing
                             but at least you are earning

DOLARES

   the currency of success
     of security
    of upward mobility

         how long can this last
         what retirement fund
          what tax returns

for all the things I heard my parents say and for all
they kept in silence
I honor their   sweat
               blood
               tears

I am not ashamed
for I am a product of their sacrifices

I'll probably bleed at the Border ™

Last time, I wept
and those tears followed me
Made me a stranger in my own body
Pushing and pulling
Until I dissected the cemetery that had sprouted

A swelling scar
Man-made
Groomed
Occupied by military
Invades natural habitats
Deterring the flow of migration

As long as the border remains
I'll count the faces, not just the black bags
traveling amongst the Pacific Ocean's waves

Which side is the other side, again?
Let's see where my blood stains…

La Trenzuda

Afternoon. Post-apocalyptic Amerikkka. A woman in her 20-30's sits next to a vanity with a brush and ribbon getting ready for war.

What are you? Yeah, you. Are you made of muscles and tendons? Is your heart beating? Does your breath get heavy when you're sad? Do you eat your mother's food with joy like I do? Do you ache when brown and black babies cry, like I do? Let me listen to your heart. No. I guess I'm not human enough if you keep putting up walls, decorating them with barbed wire. Are you free? Can you give some to me? Just a little bit. If you can't throw me a piece, can you at least describe it? What does it smell like— like magnolias in April? My nostrils don't cooperate. They've become mute from the plastic I inhale. What does it taste like— like sweet fruit picked from a tree? I get mine indoors. Chew the rubbery top layer. Wash it down with tap lead poisoned water to no avail. What does it feel like—like running wild across a field? I wish I could remember how to run but my limbs are forgetting how to bend.

she starts to run her hair through her fingers, then with a brush

Abuelito tells me about corn fields and curses Salina's NAFTA deals under his breath. They call me gringa for being born on this side of the border but my body is indigenous. Short and maciza, the kind that doesn't sell beauty products in magazines.

she demonstrate her hands, then continues to brush

You see my brown hands, foreign, a warning sign. Why? Are you afraid they will form fists and revolt? What do you have to gain from suppressing my freedom? Does this excite you, to hold me back, to shove discipline and assimilation down my throat till I'm too dizzy and ashamed to talk to my family in their tongues? You point at me and call me anchor baby not knowing how mighty this anchor has grown to be. Sustaining loved ones while also reaching for monarch butterflies. Asking them to sing the hymns of my ancestors, to stop my tears from flowing.

she begins to braid her hair

The 14th amendment written in quill and paper didn't include my brown hands. Treaty of Guadalupe Hidalgo was a farce. How dare you use the sacred names Guadalupe and Hidalgo for your political advantage. Mendez vs Westminster desegregated us wetbacks but in my grade school honors classes, it hardly felt like inclusion when white kids spat at me, called my long black braids ugly. Now I choose to grow them long. Tie them up into trenzas, toss them around for self-defense and self-preservation. You say you stand for justice but we know the law bends backwards to defend white men. While black and brown, queer, diaspora, refugee, indigenous, disabled have fought for what you boast about. Give credit where credit is due. I have hope for a future when your parades and statues will celebrate their resilience, when the fourth of July won't sound like Aleppo or Palestine because we won't have to assert our superiority over others. I will survive and so will the next generation, whether we were meant to be free or not. I tell my mother I dream of running wild in fields. I may be gaining back my sense of smell. I'm on a journey. One where I carry love because that's all I have room for in my pockets. I'll teach my legs how to run and I won't stop till I can smell magnolias and eat real fruit. Then I will learn how to liberate my people.

misogyny invites itself in with a joke

sits down next to your father, brother, cousin
plays a game of who can make you more uncomfortable
begs to be given the benefit of the doubt
when you leave will text, *miss you*
when you don't come back
will put out a missing person's report
make itself the victim
turn you into the villain

you will see this unfold
put a piece of yourself on the sidewalk
in case someone misses you
it will wash away within an hour
as the water rises
you will be left with no other choice:
find balance in your elements
vulnerability, rage, doubt
fight back
—or drown

I forgot to ask my therapist

What do you do when you find the map, search for the treasure and dig up your traumas? Do you cover it back up? Or do you take them out gently? Cut them like meat, season them with salt and lay them out to dry. And what do you do with the holes you dug? How do you not fall back into them when they are part of the trail? Do you leave them exposed? Or feed the emptiness? You're good at playing the martyr, but will those approaching eat you for supper or fall in with you?

When you asked me how I'm doing
did you expect a one word answer?

HALT

H
A
L
T
stands for
Heavenly Alternative Lethargic Time
or
Hey Actually Lets Tomorrow
or
Half A Leftover Thai food
or
Hold A Laugh Tightly

In the middle of a panic attack
hands shaking
cheeks wet
it's hard to focus

hungry, check
angry, check
lonely, check
tired, check

I have to remember
I don't want to hurt myself
I don't want to let go

guilty

of hitting refresh
of not picking up after the mess
of being a chillona
of having feelings
of projecting out to the world

I would be lying if I told you I didn't feel as empty as a miscarriage

Baby
Honey
Sweetie
What's up with the attention seeking
the binge eating
the guilt freaking
the air venting
the candid posing

What's worse, getting your roots cut out
or your words
if in one you lose your nourishment
and in the other your aesthetics

What's up with your fam bam
your slam jam
your cancer crab
your lusting man

Eres o te haces

You still singing
still dancing
still waiting for applause that won't come
still getting up early
still waiting for a new moon
still meditating on the bus
still counting your blessings
still feeling those earth tears
still picking yourself up
you still there?

endurance

morning
the soil feels wet
my bare feet are grounded like a tree
I set my intention
    mid-day
        the sun rays remind me to keep going
        sweat drips down my face
        as I wring a bandana with my blistering fingers
    I feel my arm get tense
    Throw my machete to the ground
    I remain resolute
        Far from glamorous appeal and soulless monotony
        Sounds of a river are heard
        With a richness of wisdom that whispers to me
    I would rather cut through this jungle
    To find my own path
    Than follow in anyone else's
        night falls
        have visions of where this path will take me
I wake up knowing
this is the right path
because it's mine

manifesto

2017 — the year that I finally embraced being called a bitch. because I know what they are saying behind my back or under their breath. *she's nice but then she has her moments.* Yes! I am that bitch. that rolls her eyes. unfollows your email thread. says it like it is. calls in sick to emotional labor. won't think twice about smacking that smirk off your petty ass face. sticks to her budget. says, show me don't tell me. won't take your apology as a change of heart. knows better than to blame herself for everything. won't change her mind to please you. leaves the group chat. keeps you on read because she has too many things to do and you are not one of them. refuses to put down the pen. I will take it further than what Tina Fey once said. bitches don't just get stuff done. bitches are gonna turn this world upside down, inside out, hold em by the legs to claim the change we've been working for. And I hope today as you read these words, the bitch in you recognizes the bitch in me.

document it

the art thing   the ripped books of anti-immigrant narratives thing
the resistance thing   the building something from crumbs things
the talk back thing   the generational trauma
the display of places gone thing   folded in 8 ×11 thing

the coming home thing
the homies who submit thing
the not only white men can be in galleries thing
the scoot over so my ma can see me in the back row thing
I ask myself
what's the difference
between surviving and thriving
but maybe what I'm pondering is
how many days I am surviving
I answer before the thought escapes my mouth
seven days a week

beauty is in the eye of my beloved

the spanish coming out of the corners of my mouth
are my parents peeking in to say good morning

the pelos on my arms and brows
are my grandma protecting me from harsh sun rays

the twinkle in my brown eyes
is my grandfather's smile

the brown skin you cringe at
is my connection to the cosmos

and for every revolution around the sun
I can't help but grow

unapologetically

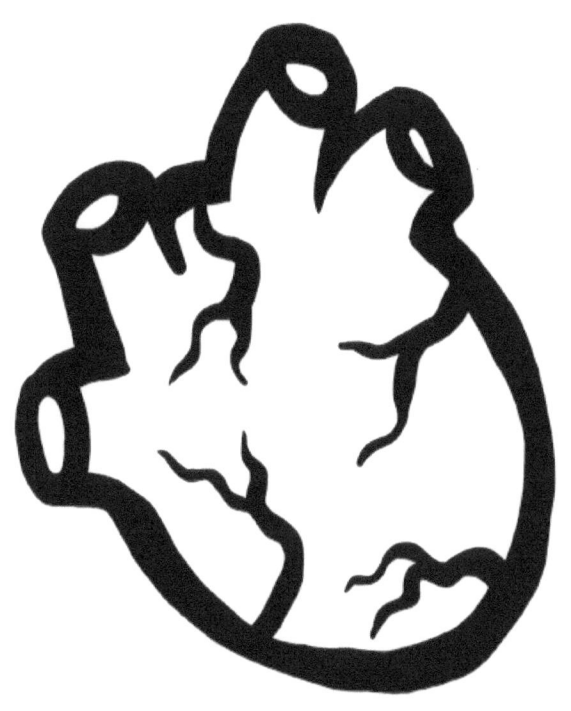

Heart
noun.
a hollow muscular organ that pumps the blood through the circulatory system by rhythmic contraction and dilation[1]; the part you are told to protect in theory, but theories are always tested; the organ humans blame for making thoughtless decisions.

craving citrus

It took as long as it took to peel an orange to realize that I love you
thick like the walls of my heart can be
It was a difficult task

my fingernails stung
rind stabbed me

couldn't contain myself
I began to eat
my tastebuds recognized poignant zest
your image appeared in my head

you left me

Bittersweet

how to have a good cry

In times of self-care juice cleanses and trivial affirmations, I fear there is not enough information circulating amongst today's overachieving, underpaid, millennials on how to have a good ol' snotty cry. This tutorial is designed for all ages and skill levels.

Disclaimer: Spirit may take over in the most unfortunate of circumstances so it is your responsibility to take care of yourself.

Tools you will need:
- your physical body
- your emotional body
- tissues

Optional items strongly encouraged:
- mirror
- something cozy to comfort yourself (ie. blanket, bed, pet)

Steps:

1. Pick an excuse to be alone. Get creative but be practical.
2. Time is of the essence. Start immediately.
3. If you haven't started crying, move your body. The body stores emotions in places like the throat and the hips.
4. If this doesn't work—bitch you're emotionally constipated.
      This will take several sessions. Don't get discouraged.
5. Look at yourself in the mirror. This is a crucial step as you get more experienced. Observe the kind of tears that have emerged. With time you will learn how to interpret them.
6. Clean up with tissues. Breathe. Meditate or nap if necessary. Congratulate yourself for feeling.

Pink Lights Up

Sunset. Ausencia, a woman in her 40's or older, sits at a dining room table next to a stranger who knocked on her door about an environmental survey. She is imagining something else.

Give me the venom. Give me the vile. Softly. It smells like lavender and I want to taste it. I'm thirsty for beauty. I have none of it left and the earth is dying. Look outside. Look at them. The beds of clouds, the purple and pink in the sky that looks right out of a Gene Kelly classic. Perfect. Too perfect to be true? You want to know why? Because they're actually gases that have polluted the air. Yeah, we are all just dying against a pretty backdrop. No one cares about the environment. Beauty sells, kid. And I have run out of money. What else is a woman to aspire to if not their beauty? The silky white hair, snow white skin, eyes like the ocean. My eyes are black. Like mud. My hair stringy like cheese. My mouth is dry.

Give me the venom! I don't remember the last time I laughed or had innocent dreams. I have no passion to cook or sing or skip around dusting this shack. And what else is a woman to do, but give her life and worldly talents to a man? They have all left me. Each one with a crying bundle in arms. For a long time I was consoled that at least beauty would not leave me. That as long as I had enough for my pencil skirts and stiletto nails and eyelash extensions I didn't need a man. But I was weak. I risked it all. And for what? So my babies could be taken away? So I could sell my body to the night? I made one friend in all these years that stayed loyal— her name is regret. She greets me every morning. She reminds me that I'm on house arrest and that I will never get back what I once had. Give me the venom. I plead you. You don't know what these eyes have seen. If I die I want to go beautifully. Intoxicated with artificial flavoring. With the taste I once had for life.

mojito

she handed me the drink
it was sweating
as if it was afraid I would waste it on a treacherous man

the mint painted the glass
and I remembered all the times nature saved my life
the crystal felt heavy
so I let it anchor me down

the bar bench was sticky and the room was loud
but I could finally think straight
everyone around me moved in slow motion
maybe they could read the heartbreak on my chest

I emptied the glass
still I didn't feel full
because I knew it was over

dis en tangled

up I drift like a helium balloon
      how often my strings have made knots
untying myself from those cable chords
      rising to new heights
only to land alone in the polluted waters

    focus
      It's too early to know
will this antigravity experience be corresponded
      I accept the adventure
If only for this moment
      keep a rock in my pocket for safety
I'm itching to let go

without over apologizing

I'm sorry my ocean waves are too strong to be anchored
    I've had to provide
        my own source of warmth for so long

I forgot how to hold someone's hand
    water comforts me so I'd rather be lost at sea
        with no reflection than find myself in your eyes

    they say hurt people
        find comfort in their loneliness
            so darling

                this distance is all the love I can give you

    Though I may leave a bad taste in your mouth
        you won't speak of me for long
            perhaps

            you may only hear me
            as a soundbite
                in the soundtrack of your life

I improvised a monologue

    it went something like,
        "I don't have resting bitch face, that's just my face"
    remember looking at him when i said,
        "men—you can't just tell me to smile. you
        have to earn it.
        make me laugh".
    he did. for a long second.

    I guess I should've been more specific and asked,
        "can you make me laugh for longer
        than men have made me cry?"

    he likes impermanent, permanence though
    which is fine
    explains why he asked to take my best friends picture
    and not mine
    and why to this day it's one of my favorite pictures of her
    she was all joy and no smile

stop raising him, he's not your son

the problem with men
losing themselves in my eyes is
they'll never find what they're looking for

they'll call me angelic
until I act foolish
then bash me for sending mixed signals
they'll call me talented
until I cannot juggle anymore
then reject me for deceiving them

how dare I
know myself better than they know
the tears that come from their eyes

what they're searching for
they lost
a long time ago
and I cannot be their childhood toy
their scratched up CD
their favorite blanket

I almost wish I had a sign that said: keep your melancholy to yourself

if their eyes wanted to dance with my soul
so badly

they would need to learn a whole new rhythm

and how can I trust someone
who doesn't know the beat
of their own wound
half man half pixels that come in and out of focus
with a hunger
I cannot fill

there is no other way to put this gently
in no language
will this sound sweet

the last fuckboi

	ran out of excuses and socks
and like	has an empty fridge, and pockets full of regrets
so, yeah	will attempt being nice one more time before he decides to end it all
and	by the end, he means: delete social media and start new accounts
dude	forgets if he's already slept with her or some one with a similar face
totally	gets triggered at concerts
for sure	takes his partner for granted
definitely	doesn't have his daughter's phone number

La Sirena

Evening. Sierra has received her first care package from Josephine and in return must hold her end of the deal by trying to recall what she remembers from her last days as a human.

I know I'm supposed to remember what happened, but I just don't, okay. Tal vez I don't want them to know the truth of who he was. Ruben was just a shapeshifter. Underneath that hard exterior there was a tortured soul with no real home. A man persecuted by humans, hunted by his own shadows, cornered by his own demise. He caught wave of how I moved. My gestures, my quirks, my rhythm until we danced one night till the sun came up. Caray, I felt like were twin flames. I learned to care for him so deeply. I didn't know that I could put all my energy and time into loving one person like that. He had me engrossed. Envuelto en su dedo. I could not let him go. It was so invigorating because he meant so much to so many people. I felt indispensable to the movement in a way. Everything was for his love. But he did not look at me as his equal, as his compañera en la lucha. No. I was his prey.

He was the cool vato that whispered sweet nothings to all the girls. Oh he was good with his words. You should have met this valiente. He knew how to rile up la gente. He had this bravado that grew crowds anywhere we went. He always spoke about the dangers that laid out there. About the peligros and the lies and the thieves hidden within the system. So I never thought he was the one to look out for.

One day he told me he had something to tell me so we went for a walk around campus. I asked him where we were but he just grew real close to me. My heart was racing. He placed his fingers under my chin, caressed my face and looked me deep in the eyes. I didn't even notice when he began to smother me until I was gasping for air. Instincts kicked in and I scratched him. Dug my fingers deep into his face. I went for his eye but he slapped my hand away. That's when I fell to the ground and hit my head. I could see blood in my reflection but I didn't know where it had come from. I tried to drag myself away from him. Looked up only to see no trace of pity or remorse. I screamed so loud but even with the echo in this chamber no one could hear me outside. I yelled anyways and cried, "¡auxilio!" He hit me with his foot and before I could react I was in the chlorinated water. I didn't know how to swim. He knew that. As I tried to hold on to the edge of the pool he told me, "you're worthless". I yelled at him, "not even to you? I gave you everything and still I mean nothing to you?" He responded with one last shove with what felt like all of his strength. I sank. And I disintegrated into tiny bits at the bottom of this pool. Taking up as little space as possible, even after death. But some pieces of me survived. It took a while, but I'm here again. And you're the first person to see me—like this.

breaking patterns, leaving notes

The next time a man says, I love you
I want you to reply with
thanks, I love me too

If he gets offended or makes fun of you
your light intimidates him
leave before he breaks you

at times you must protect yourself from people
simply because you've learned the incredible things your love can do
and *that shit ain't for the faint of heart*

and if they want to go, let them out through the back alley
only good guests are allowed to ring the bell
love yourself with the passion you have for sticky notes and statement outfits
make yourself a zine and put your face on the cover
exfoliate with apricot seed oil and coffee grounds
turn it into a ritual to honor the women that have had sleepless nights for you
love yourself for the words they are still finding meaning to
how beautiful you are empty and full
don't forget to be generous with yourself
put the fires out with lemon and pomegranate juice
and if loving yourself is a mistake
let if be the most spectacular mistake you make

mosaic

My favorite number is zero
like the swirl of a latte
or when you forget my name
but not my face
my favorite symbol is infinity
like the possibilities laid out in front of me
and picking one in a thousand
what are the chances we would meet
my favorite cafe smell
one that comes after you leave
the pastry on your sweater
spiced chai between your teeth
my favorite memory is this moment
already becoming history
nothing and everything exist
over and over
until you sit down and realize
nothing is under control
tears will come without tissues
poems will come without paper
lovers will meet without words
songs will be sung with not sound
art will be made
without borders
and you will
take a chance
bet

and if it fails
    it only lasts a lifetime
    I mean a moment
    they are all one and the same you see
        because even if there was
        a manual on life
    someone would not go by the book
so what if no one recognizes you
so what if you're the odd one out
so what if your dreams do not exist yet
all along you knew
  the trick was
dedication
surrender
all along
you knew you could start from zero
    all along you knew that no matter how hard
        you mess up
            what's meant for you
            will always find its way
    some day
  in a classroom
someone may want
  to analyze these words
  only to find out
    they aren't even mine
      all I did was sit down
        drink tea like any other day

this poem was written
long before I was born
it just so happened that today
I was ready for more
than a fleeting moment

heart

I don't know if it's spring
summer or fall here

but it's definitely
raining and humid

quite uncomfortable but I'm placing
buckets to catch the water

for when my poems go dry

Head
noun.
a compact mass of leaves or flowers at the top of a stem, the upper part of the human body[1]; the part ancestors wrote about to signify the spirit. What you are told to protect in an earthquake—because no one deserves to hold any more trauma.

shedding

I couldn't even look in the mirror
at the horror
my body did not belong to me
I had lost all contact with myself
outgrown the skin I was in
afraid of what I would find beneath
I began to peel the layers off
what surfaced was pain
heartache and confusion
grief over a stage in my life
My eyes felt heavy
head was dizzy
sometimes I tried to hide it
but there was no turning back
As soon as my pores began to regain oxygen
my limbs quickly worked
to get out of my old skin
I remember the day
when I could smile in the mirror again
I could speak without regret
I call it an in-body experience
because often
the answer isn't outside
isn't it funny
how sometimes
the most difficult place to go
is within

Y SI NO ME QUIEREN

A One-Womxn Play

CHARACTERS
ELLA: a college student, stubborn, short, not a typical beauty, currently reading Anzaldua, questioning her chingona-ness

TIME
The present, morning.

PLACE
A living room that transforms into places and spaces of her memory.

SCENE 1
Open It

ELLA

Good morning. What do we have on our agenda today? Call the bank about that overdraft fee from your student loan? Boring. Take out the sewing machine and finish the project you've been saying you've been working on for months? Too much effort. Revisit all the haters you've had and go down a deep hole of remembrance and peeling away at the layers of life even though it won't serve you any good and actually make you feel less motivated than you already feel? hmm sounds intriguing.

> *She takes out a manila folder with*
> *HATE MAIL written on it*
> *She is swept by memories of her childhood*
> *Echos*
> *do like the animals do…*
> *como la flor*
> *WHATEVER YOU SAY GOES BACK TO YOU!!!*
>
> *she is being punched, shoved, hair pulled*

VOICES (offstage)
What's your name?

> *softly*

ELLA
ella

VOICES (offstage)
What?

ELLA
ell-a

VOICES (offstage)
What's she saying teacher? Look, she's gonna start crying again!

ELLA
My name is ELLA!! Now can you hear me?

She comes back to the present

ELLA
These days, I carry an agenda. A pen, in my pocket like you do.
I don't know when I'll see you again. So I wish that this time you not interrupt me. Look at me. We have a history, remember?
As a child I would hug you and try to catch your attention.
You never more than smirked at my love offerings.
You see, the day you took the training wheels off my bike,

Was the first day you took my love for granted.
You expected nothing but the best from me.
Nothing but obedience. And obedient I was. The
world is your enemy and everyone was at fault for
what happened to you. What happened to you?
You would sit on the couch, prop up your feet and
felt like you owned everything. Your neck stretched
so half the time you wouldn't even glance at me. And
when you heard bad news and saw me mumbling
you would send me to the room.

There I learned to trace the shadow of the desk,
for I was in that room receiving my punishment. I
screamed and cried and I could hear the pounding in
my head and my heart racing and my back burning
from the beating. You would leave the house, and my
screaming would turn into silent weeping. I would
slowly get up and walk to the bathroom where my
mother and sister were hiding and crying. Shaking,
my mother said, "tu papá te quiere" but in my head
I thought: If that is love, then I don't want to love
anyone.

I know what love means now. Love fed me, and I
bathed in love and I slept with love and dreamt with
love. I do. I want to share it with the world. I want
everyone to know what real love feels like. The day
you took my training wheels off my bike, you let me
learn a big lesson. The tables have certainly turned.

Because now you send me birthday cards and flowers and I just don't have the time. You see, I carry an agenda with me, and a pen…like you do. You wanted your freedom so badly, so now for once don't be selfish and let me have mine. Look at me father. Straight in the eye. For the words I've spoken might pain you, but these tears I wear are of release. Because never in my life will I have to trace the shadow of the desk again. I have love to thank for that.

END SCENE

SCENE 2
The Letter

She reveals another letter

ELLA
Ahh, one of my favorite hate letters
*She recites the words
in a girly voice*
Dear Ella. We are writing to you because we have something to tell you. Once you finish reading this letter please don't talk to us. We have agreed that we don't want to be your friend anymore because we hate you. We hate you and your whole family, except your mom. She's cool. Anyway. We never want to talk to you or be your friend.
Good-bye forever. Mailee and Yessica
*rolling up her sleeves
and pretends to take off
her earrings to respond*
Dear Mailee and Yessica. Thank you. I don't want to be your friend either. And my mom doesn't like you so -ha. I wrote about your little letter in my admissions to college and I got in!
Guess who's laughing now?
*Luna Lunita song starts
she sings a song to the moon*

*Luna lunita
Luna que linda*

te apareces de nuevo
te apareces de nuevo
no tengo razones
para sentirme triste por las noches
no tengo razones
para sentirme sola al caminar
porque estarás ayi
porque estarás ayi
cuando miro al cielo
estarás ahí
Luna lunita
que bien te miras
gracias por ser mi amiga
Luna lunita
que bien te miras
gracias por ser mi amiga

END SCENE

SCENE 3
Beauty Hurts

Ella sits surrounded by beauty products

ELLA
My mom always told me, la belleza cuesta mijita.
Plucks an eyebrow
Ow. Gotta do my hair, gotta do my eyebrows, gotta do my squats. Gotta do my hair, gotta do my eyebrows, gotta do my —ugh squats
Does squats while plucking
eyebrows and takes out
a curling iron
while she does lunges

Enough!
Que tal si no quiero ser bonita
Si lo que quiero es
Respeto
Dignidad
Amor Sincero
gritar a los cuatro vientos
Libertad
Mi silencio no lo compran con halagos o soborno
No me reduzcan a un poem, una pintura
Mírame
Soy de carne y hueso
No me digan que calladita me veo mas bonita
porque eso me da más fuerzas para alzar la voz

sus ideas falsas de belleza no se miden contra el poder de mi palabra
El mar es bello, la guitarra es encantadora, el viento es místico
Porque no se callan
¿Por qué no se callan?

END SCENE

SCENE 4
Peeling Oranges

Ella begins peeling an orange and putting the peels in clear container filled with water and rose petals

ELLA

Once in a while
I'll think of you
and then scold myself
For how I let you shame and mock me
drowning as I asked for help
How you kept me on edge giving me a regular dose
of your venom
I drank it because it reminded me of home
I know you're addicted to the pain
because at some point you became so numb
You'd get jealous whenever i saw
a mirage of hope
My mind gets foggy with rage
As I hear about your
Wandering
Lusting for warmth at the expenses of others
boundaries
It ain't worth it, it ain't worth it
Now as I sink deep into my alter
I give thanks for having learned the repulsive taste of abuse

although it may look and smell like rosewater

*She puts on a beanie and
adjusts her posture to slouch*

I used to have a boyfriend. He wasn't extraordinarily handsome or an intellectual genius. He was just really really kind and I really admired him for that. We had a wonderful relationship—kind of. We broke up. In short terms he cheated on me. Turns out she was taller than me and skinnier than me and white, blond hair blue eyes the whole thing. That did a lot of damage to my self esteem and to my pansa. I showed him my pansa. I showed him my ribcage which is like the unsexiest worst part of my body I think. I've never liked it, I've hated it in fact. But then I realized I come from short maciza women— laborers, who worked out in fields. And I love them as they are. And they love me. So, I'm gonna learn how to love me. And I'm gonna learn how to love my pansa— no matter the size.

END SCENE

SCENE 5
Can't Touch Me

Ella sits on a desk in class

PROFESSOR (offstage)
Due to our political climate and in consideration of some students who have expressed discomfort in the classroom I would like to make it clear that politics is not to be discussed here. Leave your opinions at the door.

ELLA
If the US is so ready for Trump as President, they better be ready to meet me at an all time Chingona, Cabrona, Sinvergüenza, high.
Like my grandma who threw rocks and punches at a guy who tried to assault her, high
Like my great-grandmas and tias who raised children and worked en el campo, high
Like my grandma
I will throw rocks and punches
I will rise up
I will not be defeated
Like my great-grandmas and tias
I will raise my voice
I will sing my hymn
I will drink in the sun and moon which you will never privatize
Tus palabras

Tus miradas
Tus gestos
No me tocan
Defiendo mi palabra
Mi grito que es mio
Mi resistencia
Mi forma de sanar
Digas lo que digas
Yo no me rajo
I don't give up
Chingona, Cabrona y más alerta que nunca

END SCENE

SCENE 6
My Favorite Hater

ELLA

Well, that was fun. I guess there's nothing left in here. Nope. All done.

She shakes the notebook and one last letter falls out

Oh, shit.

She opens it

Hello, we meet again. You selfish piece of crap. You cynical, crybaby. You two faced fake, manipulative, self-sabotaging…
NO! I—I can't do this again. Damnit, I'm exhausted.

She breaks the fourth wall addressing the audience

What happens when you stop hiding from yourself and dedicate the hours to finding light in the darkest rooms
vibrate with sound and pour water
Stand with intention and not regret
Because you chose to come out of your jail
Surely it was worth the mis steps you made
which led you here
where you need to be
a step closer to freedom
We love to obsess about the people that hate us.
We give them all our attention. But we rarely give

attention to all of those who show up, who've picked us up, who've taught us how to dance. Who show us they give a damn.

END SCENE

SCENE 7
Resignation

She tears up the hate mail
addresses the audience

ELLA

This is for anyone who is tired of trying to be perfect
Open your hands
untie your mind
You are better because you are not perfect
That's why you've laughed and cried
Because you are a feeling human being
Your mind plays tricks on you
When it tells you to be ashamed of who you are
You are not behind
You are where you need to be in your journey
Perfection, after all, is how people sell products
a better life, sex, food, fame
But all of those things will not liberate you from the
pain of feeling inadequate in your own skin
You are not perfect
and you don't have to be
in order to live a full life
in order to be worthy
Y si no me quieren, and if they don't like me?
Y si no me aceptan, and if they don't accept me?
Y si me dejan, if they leave me?
Y si no cumplen con su palabra, if they don't follow

through with their word?
Pues
Yo me quiero. Yo me acepto. Yo me mantengo firme.
Yo cumplo con mi palabra.
I love me. I accept me. I stand by me. I keep my word.
trying to convince herself
Y si no me quieren, yo me quiero
attempting to be louder
Y si no me quieren, yo me quiero
affirming
Y si no me quieren, yo me quiero

END OF PLAY
LIGHTS OUT

to this body

                         I used to hide
                behind my mother's smile
            her pain like a boulder I pushed
      her stories extending out of my fingertips
I used to think my mother's face was mine

                       My heart lived
          in her heart
             —just until I found a better place

                              Some people
                     call this empathy
            I call it time travel
         Be careful, my bruja friend told me once
So if I may
        I would like to address her
        with the tenderness she's always wanted

—para mi cuerpo

You have survived
Both physical and emotional brutality
Stretched and shrunk
But refused to be taken for granted
With every ache and sore
You cry out, love me

I'm listening
I'm sorry it took so long
But I'm tuning in

I didn't want her to die

I kept watering her
even after you'd disappointed me
even after strangers smelled grief on my clothes
I laughed it off,
oh how I exercise this muscle called my face

I took the last petal home with me
placed it between two pages of an old journal
hoping maybe she would grow again
if she was reminded
she'd survive this too

we all knew her sentence
yet that naive sense in me
pinned my mouth to the floor
no more

in the distance
a person
screaming
I felt nothing but the dry heat of
an overstimulated engine

fragile
delicate
paper thin spine
once she was all skeleton

when she needed her
rotten roots cut off
I did it
to remind her
there is life after

ya no conspires ni suspires
solamente respira, corazón
stop conspiring and holding
your breath for others
just breath, cariño
that's all you have to do

there's a cumbia in here for you

nothing says fuck
the
patriarchy
like
taking yourself
out
              changing   the music
              in the empty dancehall
              swinging   your belly
              Free
              muévelo   muévelo
                      y alto
sweat pulsing gently
      framing your temples
your back and crown
      judgement subsides
skirt hugs your thighs
      hips riding sound waves
accenting the beat

a white man calls
Wepa
You read their lips
Wetback

frozen
mid turn

in the mirror
you are
sequinless
arrhythmic
drenched
in mockery
a caricature
of your choice
Santa o Puta
but before knees lock
your arms untangle
fists unclench

            You are not   an imposter
            You are not   an imposter
            You are   tenochtitlán
            You are   tepoztlán
            You are   chilacachapa

a whole fucking kingdom
to care and protect

call it joy

when the sun doesn't acknowledge
your accomplishments
that's when you really shine
when the spotlight is no longer on you
but you've got one more dance
in your bones
wiggle it out
exchange that intimate movement
with another human
ask the lecturer a question they don't
know the answer to
watch it take flight
bumping with everything around taunting
no one is the expert

don't tell me there is none left
then why do flowers keep
humming in a storm
why does the squirrel keep
looking for peanuts in my plants
why do people stop to count stars until
they are out of numbers

don't you think
there might be
—yes even for us
just a little bit left

evolving

Muscle memory on point
    Affirmations on deck
        Self love rituals on rotation

I'm making space to create

        Clearing path to find serenity in solitude
            Knowing some people won't be able to keep up
                Because this growth won't wait for anyone

            I'm transforming
                My foundation is in a rupture
                    Growing pains have shaken me

The seeds I've planted are meeting the sun

                So I stretch every morning
                Walk with intuition
                    Sit with gratitude

              I cut the rope that tied me
to unravel
                    and weave over
        The patterns that caused me harm
      I know to get out of my own way this time
    Nothing can stunt my growth
  This isn't even my final form

for folks that are soft

balance your body with song
push in to let out sound
and release the shame
that invaded your home

walk away
let them whisper
they will always have critiques
and you will always have substance

once you stop listening to the static
the messages will come
you have everything
when you recognize your power

drop the baggage you've held for others
put the lesson on a patch
sow it on your sleeve
and keep going

despite the world
and all it demands of you
stay soft
tender to the touch

appreciate cuddles and lavender ice cream
dance barefoot and sun bathe in the nude

make potions to clean and brew intentions
inviting hummingbirds to break bread

mi abuela se sabe una canción

atiende su jardín como conductora de sinfónica
nota quien anda desafinado
quien no anda de buenas esta mañana
les corrige y despierta hasta que listos
practican una canción
¿como una viejita sin estudio puede crear tan bellas melodías?
preguntan los vecinos

no entienden que
cuando alguien crece entre el frijol y el elote
se aprende un canto muy distinto al de la ciudad
que hasta guitarristas profesionales no lo pueden interpretar

my grandma knows a song

treats her garden like a symphony conductor
notes who is out of tune
who is not in a good mood this morning
corrects and sets straight until together
they practice a song
how can an old lady with no formal education create such
beautiful melodies?
the neighbors ask

they don't understand
when someone grows amongst the bean and corn
they learn a song so different than the city folks
even professional musicians cannot interpret

una semilla

Arrancarán nuestra fruta
Arrancarán nuestro árbol
Arrancarán nuestras raíces

Pero la fruta da vida
Porque la fruta da semillas
Que aunque se rieguen
A largas distancias
Con tierra
Y con lluvia
Darán mas vida

Yo soy una semilla
Pero se de donde vine
Porque se que sin raíces no tendría vida

Arrancarán mi árbol
Arrancarán mis raíces
Pero la fruta da vida

Y la fruta da semillas
Y las semillas no se olvidan
Aunque se rieguen a largas distancias

Nos quitaran nuestra casa
Nos quitaran nuestro pueblo
Nos quitaran nuestros lenguajes

Nos quitaran nuestras costumbres

Pero a largas distancias
Con tierra
Y con lluvia
Las semillas
No se olvidan

Porque sin raíces
No hay vida

community call-in
TeAda Productions song 2017

From the roots to the core to the heart to the head
From the roots to the core to the heart to the head
From the roots to the core to the heart to the head
From the roots to the core to the heart to the head
        Can I extend myself?
                take care of yourself
        I've overextended
                be careful
        Can I extend myself?
                take care of yourself
        I've overextended
                be careful
From the roots to the core to the heart to the head
From the roots to the core to the heart to the head
From the roots to the core to the heart to the head
From the roots to the core to the heart to the head
            Slow down
            Slow down
            Slow down
              Exhale

ACKNOWLEDGMENTS

First and foremost I offer respect and gratitude to Spirit and my ancestors for their love and guidance in this lifetime. Tlazocamati abuelitos Esteban y Anita. Gracias por darma su bendición. To my beautiful mother Candida, eres mi héroe y te doy las gracias por cuidarme, creer en mis sueños, y por tu empeño en sacarnos adelante. Para mi tío Carlos y mis hermanos maravillosos Xochitl & Alejandro—

I love you with all my heart y mi hígado.

To Theatre for Transformation for commissioning the original version of La Trenzuda. To the following zines and editors for publishing versions of this work: Seeds of Resistance: Flor y Canto, El Tecolote Anthology, La Bloga, FUEGO Zine. To Shruti Bala Purkayastha and the ensemble at TeAda Productions, where the song of: roots, core, heart, head was first conceptualized. To Samuel Valdez and Arinda Caballero for accepting my pitch for a solo show at the Bi-National Latinx Theater Festival which then became Y Si No Me Quieren.

This book would not be possible without the help of Sarah Rafael Garcia who has believed in my writing for over a decade and helped me develop this book. We owe you many many gorditas. Thank you to my editor Edward Vidaurre for being so supportive through the process and for the opportunity to bring me into the FlowerSong Press familia. To john jairo valencia for being an incredible friend and riding this wave of creation with me as the illustrator & illuminator of my words. I feel so privileged to know and grow with you. To Iris de Anda for being my publishing consultant and for offering her magical words to describe this book.

To all the writing advisors I've had with Barrio Writers and Barrio Actors Guild including: David Breña, Jenna Selby, David Lopez. Iuri M. Lara, Adriana Lilus, Sherine Gonzalez Solano. To Professor Angela Marino, Rosa Navarrete, Samanta Cubias, Martha Lazzaro, Juan Aldape and all the other amazing souls I met in college. To Sara Guerrero, Adriana Alba, Elizabeth Isela Szekeresh, Diana Burbano, Elvia Susana Rubalcava, Angela Estela Moore, Jacqueline Castañeda, Shanelle Garcia, Yásaman Madadi and everyone else from Breath of Fire Latina Theater Ensemble for their unwavering love and support.

To Kayleigh Levitt and the Walnut House friends for hosting me as I juggled rehearsals, late-night edits and early work schedules. To my angels Taylor and Sheri who send me gentle reminders from the spirit world that life is about showing up for the moment. To the Batocabes for taking us in when we needed it the most. To Christine, Janel, Jennifer and Fernanda for being generous, gracious, uplifting friends who saw potential in me before I could see it. To anyone who has ever helped me, advocated for me, cheered me on, and offered advice through the process of this book. And lastly, to anyone who is able to take something from reading my words. This is for you. I hope you feel inspired to share your talents and creativity with the world.

Anatalia Vallez

writer, performer and artivist from Orange County, California (Acjachemen land) and roots from Guerrero, Mexico, Anatalia is passionate about using art as a tool for creating consciousness and community. Addressing everything from migration, machismo and our relationship to nature, she seeks to find intimate truths and plant seeds to change the world. First published in Barrio Writers at seventeen, she's taken writing workshops with Las Dos Brujas, Winter Tangerine, Breath of Fire Latina Theater Ensemble and through CREAR Studio's DIY MFA program. She has a BA in Sociology and minor in Theater and Performance Studies from UC Berkeley (Ohlone land). To find out more visit:
anataliavallez.com

john jairo valencia

among other things, john jairo is a mixed media artist who works primarily through illustrative drawing and creative writing. their work is inspired by stars, spirit beings, ancestors, the natural world, dreams, storytelling and decolonization. they envision their work as a prayer for transformative change and creating un mundo donde quepan muchxs mundos. john jairo identifies as queer-xicanx-colombian and grew up in la puente and boyle heights.
To find out more visit:
jhonjairoart.weebly.com

www.ingramcontent.com/pod-product-compliance
Lightning Source LLC
Chambersburg PA
CBHW031128080526
44587CB00011B/1147